CU00726491

More Creaky Limericks

Written and illustrated by Hermione Ainley

Published by Colley Books, 11 Laud's Road,

Crick, Northamptonshire, NN6 7TJ

"How's Buffy?" "I've heard that he's dead."

"And Bunty?" "Gone soft in the head."

"And Cyril? And Don?

And Percy? And Ron?"

"Let's talk about cricket instead."

I have not been mis-sold ppi;

I have not had an accident. Why,

Just because I am old,

Must these people be told

That I can spot a scam if I try?

Nowadays experts advise

The old to take more exercise.

But I think that the shock

Of a run round the block

Would undoubtedly speed my demise.

It's happened to you I am sure

And it's such an incredible bore.

You're on the top stair -

You look round everywhere -

"Now what did I come up here for?"

Let me tell you a joke that's not funny!

I'd quite like to go somewhere sunny,

And I got all inspired

But now I've retired

I've the time but I haven't the money!

I used to walk miles every day,

But now I find to my dismay

That with creaks in my knees

And a bit of a wheeze

Just around the block seems a long way.

I'm trying to love my new phone

With its apps and its cheery ring-tone,

But sometimes its cheeps

And buzzes and beeps

Make me wish it would leave me alone.

Time was we could go for a drive

For the pleasure of being alive;

With the wind in our hair

We hadn't a care,

Whereas now we just long to arrive.

Sadly I can no longer see

A lot that is right next to me,

But that far distant blob

Is no 'little brown job',

It's a gold crest way up in that tree.

These days people all seem to mumble,

Their words just come out as a jumble.

But sadly I fear

It's just me that can't hear,

So it's probably best not to grumble.

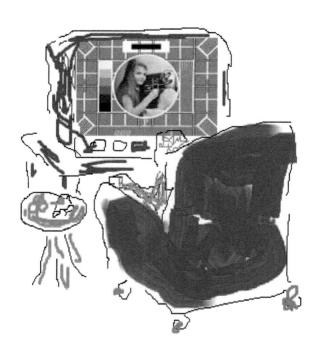

Once there was just BBC

And then along came ITV.

There's now much more choice,

At which some may rejoice,

But two channels seemed plenty to me.

I'm told that I should be down-sizing,

Which, frankly, I find patronizing.

I'm fine as I am

And I don't give a damn

For sensible reorganizing.

The grandchildren come for the day

For spoiling and sweeties and play,

But the best bit by far

Is they get in the car

And their parents just whisk them away.

I promise you I'm not a quitter!

I tried really hard to like Twitter,

But faced with such drivel

It's hard to stay civil;

I just call it Internet Litter.

There's so much advice about diet

And, if it appeals, why not try it?

But when you've had enough

Of all that healthy stuff

I suggest you give up and deep-fry it.

Dealing with bureaucracy

Is hell, I am sure we agree.

But I'll give you a hint:

The important small print

Is the bit you can no longer see.

The M1 once seemed rather fun;

The speedometer might hit the ton;

Watford Gap seemed exciting,

Yes, even inviting,

Not torture for everyone.

I once had a fine head of hair

Which was glossy and thick and quite fair,

But now it's grown thin

While the hair on my chin

Is black and sprouts up everywhere.

The pain in my shoulder is chronic.

My doctor has banned gin and tonic.

I've got to the stage

Where a happy old age

Just has to be oxy-moronic.

No I don't want a funeral plan!

I am not a considerate gran!

If there's any spare cash

I'll go out on the lash

And enjoy it all while I still can!

The End